SNOWMOBILES

Big Buddy BOOKS
Amazing Vehicles

Sarah Tieck

Amazing Vehicles

ABDO
Publishing Company

VISIT US AT
www.abdopublishing.com

Published by ABDO Publishing Company, 8000 West 78th Street, Edina, Minnesota 55439.

Copyright © 2010 by Abdo Consulting Group, Inc. International copyrights reserved in all countries. No part of this book may be reproduced in any form without written permission from the publisher. Buddy Books™ is a trademark and logo of ABDO Publishing Company.

Printed in the United States.

Coordinating Series Editor: Rochelle Baltzer
Contributing Editors: Megan M. Gunderson, BreAnn Rumsch, Marcia Zappa
Graphic Design: Deb Coldiron, Marcia Zappa
Cover Photograph: *iStockphoto.com*: ©iStockphoto.com/Shawn Lowe Photographic
Interior Photographs/Illustrations: *AP Photo*: Nathan Bilow (pp. 25, 27), Becky Bohrer (p. 7), Diana Haecker (p. 30), Angela Schneider/The Livingston Enterprise (p. 23), David Smith (p. 29), Clint Wood/Brainerd Dispatch (p. 27); *iStockphoto.com*: ©iStockphoto.com/Alpophoto (p. 13), ©iStockphoto.com/Keith Reicher (p. 21), ©iStockphoto.com/Shawn Lowe Photographic (pp. 8, 15, 25, 26); *Shutterstock*: Galina Barskaya (p. 19), Sergei Butorin (p. 7), Glen Gaffney (p. 29), Andreas Gradin (p. 5), IgorXIII (p. 11), Intra Cclique LLC (p. 9), IOFOTO (p. 7), Kwest (p. 17), Jerry Zitterman (p. 12).

Library of Congress Cataloging-in-Publication Data

Tieck, Sarah, 1976-
  Snowmobiles / Sarah Tieck.
    p. cm. -- (Amazing vehicles)
  ISBN 978-1-60453-543-3
  1. Snowmobiles--Juvenile literature. I. Title.

TL234.2.T54 2010
629.22'042--dc22

2009001760

3 1561 00232 9724

Manufactured with paper containing
at least 10% post-consumer waste

CONTENTS

Snowmobiles are sometimes called snowmachines.

GET MOVING

Imagine riding a snowmobile. Cold air chills your skin as you ride on hilly trails. You quickly cover miles of snowy, icy land.

Have you ever looked closely at a snowmobile? Many parts work together to make it move. A snowmobile is an amazing vehicle!

WHAT IS A SNOWMOBILE?

Snowmobiles are made to travel on snow and ice. They move on tracks and skis instead of wheels. So, they easily cover roads and frozen ground.

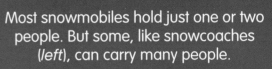

Most snowmobiles hold just one or two people. But some, like snowcoaches (*left*), can carry many people.

FAST FACT: Snowmobiles can also move on grass or pavement! In warm months, some people race on these surfaces.

Snowmobiles move quickly and easily in areas where other vehicles can't travel. They often drive off road. They travel in the **wilderness**. But, they can also go on trails or roads.

Some snowmobiles are used for **recreation**. Others are used in sports, such as racing. Some snowmobiles even help people do work.

Snowmobiles are made to ride on top of snow.

A CLOSER LOOK

A snowmobile's body is built on a frame. The frame holds the snowmobile's parts together. A snowmobile must be able to handle cold temperatures. And, it must be strong enough to travel over uneven ground.

SNOWMOBILES

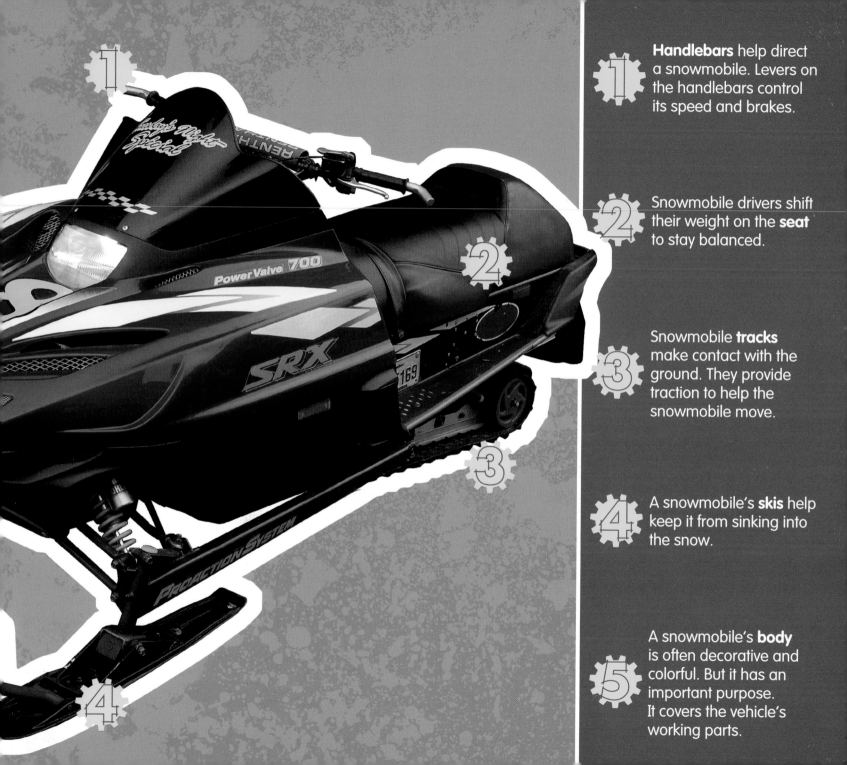

1 **Handlebars** help direct a snowmobile. Levers on the handlebars control its speed and brakes.

2 Snowmobile drivers shift their weight on the **seat** to stay balanced.

3 Snowmobile **tracks** make contact with the ground. They provide traction to help the snowmobile move.

4 A snowmobile's **skis** help keep it from sinking into the snow.

5 A snowmobile's **body** is often decorative and colorful. But it has an important purpose. It covers the vehicle's working parts.

HOW DOES IT MOVE?

Tracks allow snowmobiles to move. Most tracks have a patterned outer layer called tread. Some tracks have studs, which are small knobs that stick out of the tread. Tread and studs provide **traction**.

Inside the track, there are several wheels and **axles**. A snowmobile's engine supplies force to turn them. When the wheels turn, the track moves. This pushes the snowmobile.

Tread and studs help snowmobile tracks move over icy, uneven surfaces.

A SPECIAL ENGINE

A snowmobile's engine and transmission work together. The transmission helps send engine power to the wheels. And, it helps control the amount of engine power used.

Snowmobile transmissions are different from most vehicles. They are continuously variable transmissions (CVTs). CVTs use a **pulley** system to help control vehicle speed. They can change speeds without shifting gears.

FAST FACT: A vehicle with a standard transmission switches gears to help change speeds. The amount of engine power available changes when the vehicle switches gears.

SKI SCIENCE

Most snowmobiles have two skis. A few have only one. Skis help balance the snowmobile's weight. Their flat, smooth bottoms move easily across snow or ice.

To direct the skis, the driver turns the handlebars. The driver must also shift his or her body weight when turning the snowmobile. This keeps the snowmobile balanced.

Skis can be different lengths and widths. Wide skis allow snowmobiles to "float" on the snow. Narrow skis allow for sharper turns.

THE DRIVER'S SEAT

Snowmobiles are fun to drive. But, it takes skill to drive them safely. These machines offer little to **protect** drivers. If drivers lose control on snow and ice, they can be badly hurt.

States have different laws about who can drive snowmobiles. Some states allow young drivers who are with an adult. Others allow young drivers who have special **licenses** or have taken a safety class.

18

Most drivers wear special gear, such as snowsuits, gloves, and helmets with goggles. These protect their bodies from cold temperatures and help prevent injuries.

RIDING THE TRAILS

People often use snowmobiles for fun. They ride on trails in the snowy **wilderness**.

Snowmobiles are used in cold places around the world! Montana, Michigan, and Maine are popular places for **recreational** snowmobiling in the United States.

Sometimes people ride snowmobiles on established trails. Other times, they create new trails. Some people say this harms natural areas.

21

ON THE JOB

Some people use snowmobiles for work. Search-and-rescue workers use them to find people in snowy areas. In heavy snow, workers drive them to power lines that must be fixed. The military uses them for **combat** in cold, snowy places. And, ski resorts use them for many jobs.

Snocross events are held throughout the United States. Many times, they are in small towns near wilderness.

DARING RIDERS

Some snowmobilers ride in snocross races. In these popular events, riders speed around snowy racetracks. They make quick turns and jump over hills and bumps. They can **compete** in several different events during a season.

Snocross can be unsafe, so riders wear special gear. Body armor, helmets, and shin guards help **protect** riders.

FAST FACT: Snocross has many fans. Some fans watch the races on television. Others bundle up to attend live races.

25

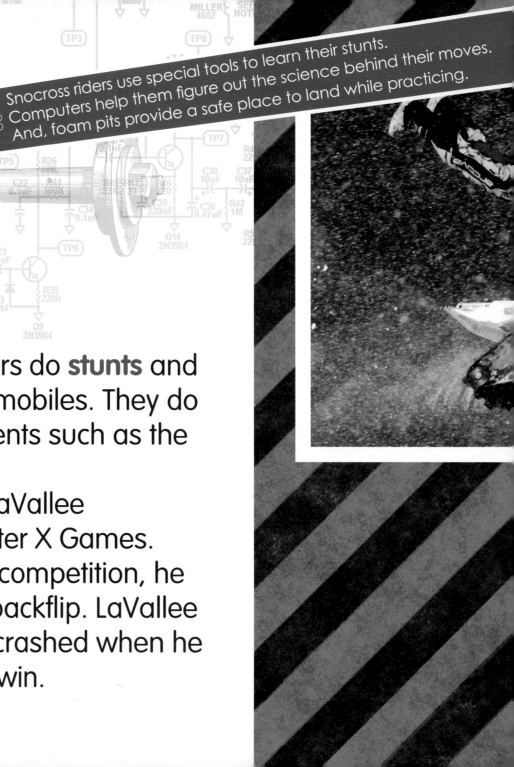

Some snocross riders do **stunts** and tricks with their snowmobiles. They do jumps and flips at events such as the X Games.

In 2009, rider Levi LaVallee **competed** at the Winter X Games. During the Next Trick competition, he attempted a double backflip. LaVallee flipped twice, but he crashed when he landed. So, he didn't win.

Levi LaVallee won two gold medals at the 2008 X Games. He won the Freestyle event. He also won the Speed & Style event.

27

PAST TO PRESENT

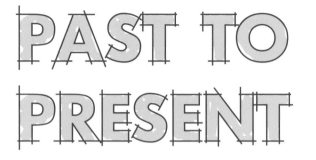

The first snowmobiles were invented during the early 1900s. Most of them were large! But in the 1950s, smaller engines were invented. This allowed Joseph-Armand Bombardier to manufacture a smaller snowmobile in 1959. This changed snowmobiles forever.

Today, more than 4 million people use snowmobiles. Some ride in races and on trails. Others use them for work, such as searching for lost people. Snowmobiles are amazing vehicles!

Early snowmobiles were made as a way to travel through snow. Today's snowmobiles are more advanced. They are used for racing, recreation, and work.

BLAST FROM THE PAST

In Alaska, the Tesoro Iron Dog has taken place every year since 1984. The race covers 1,971 miles (3,172 km). It is the longest snowmobile race in the world! Some riders may travel as fast as 100 miles (161 km) per hour.

This long-running race is a difficult ride through Alaska's snowy **wilderness**. There, riders brave winter temperatures that can reach -50°F (-46°C).

IMPORTANT WORDS

axle (AK-suhl) a bar on which a wheel or a pair of wheels turns.

combat fighting during war.

compete to take part in a competition. A competition is a contest between two or more persons or groups.

license (LEYE-suhnts) a paper or a card showing that someone is allowed to do something by law.

protect (pruh-TEHKT) to guard against harm or danger.

pulley a small wheel with a groove in the rim in which a rope or a belt moves.

recreation (reh-kree-AY-shuhn) an activity done in free time for fun or enjoyment.

stunt an action requiring great skill or daring.

traction (TRAK-shuhn) the power to hold onto a surface without slipping while moving.

wilderness (WIHL-duhr-nuhs) an area without settlers that is covered with wild plants and trees.

WEB SITES

To learn more about snowmobiles, visit ABDO Publishing Company online. Web sites about snowmobiles are featured on our Book Links page. These links are routinely monitored and updated to provide the most current information available.

www.abdopublishing.com

31

INDEX